Critters, Beasts and FLuFFieS

A Whimsical Creature Coloring Book
by author/artist
M.C.A. Hogarth

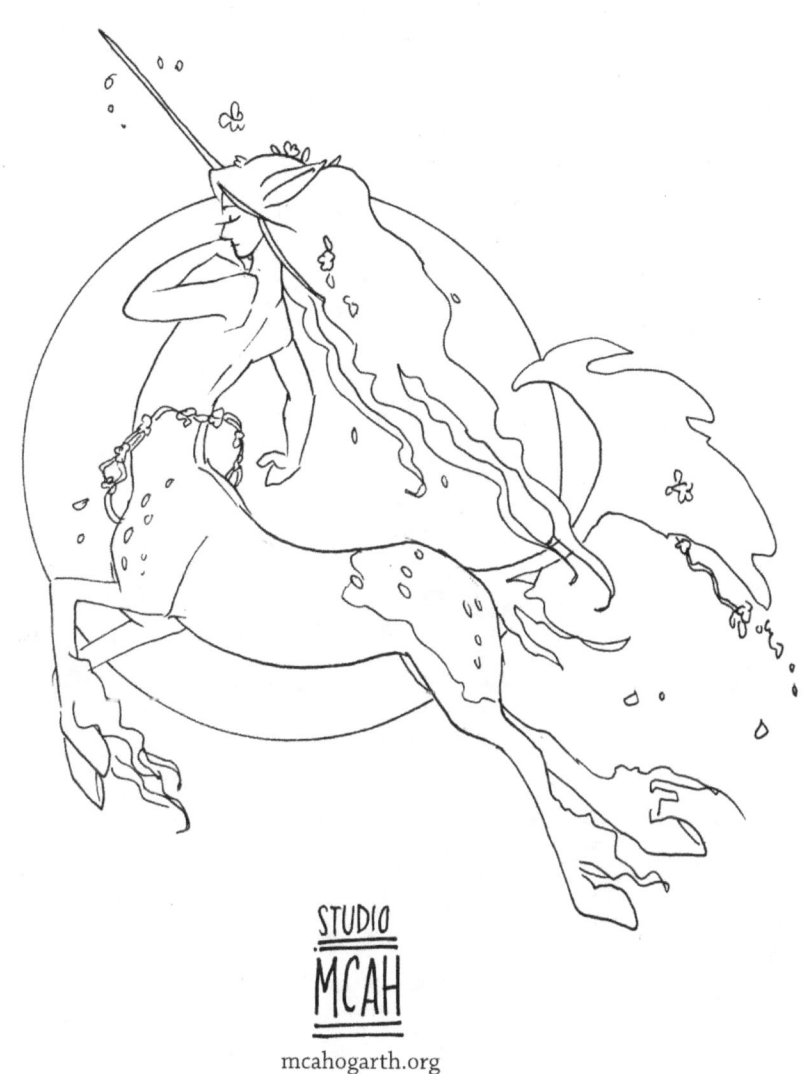

STUDIO
MCAH
mcahogarth.org

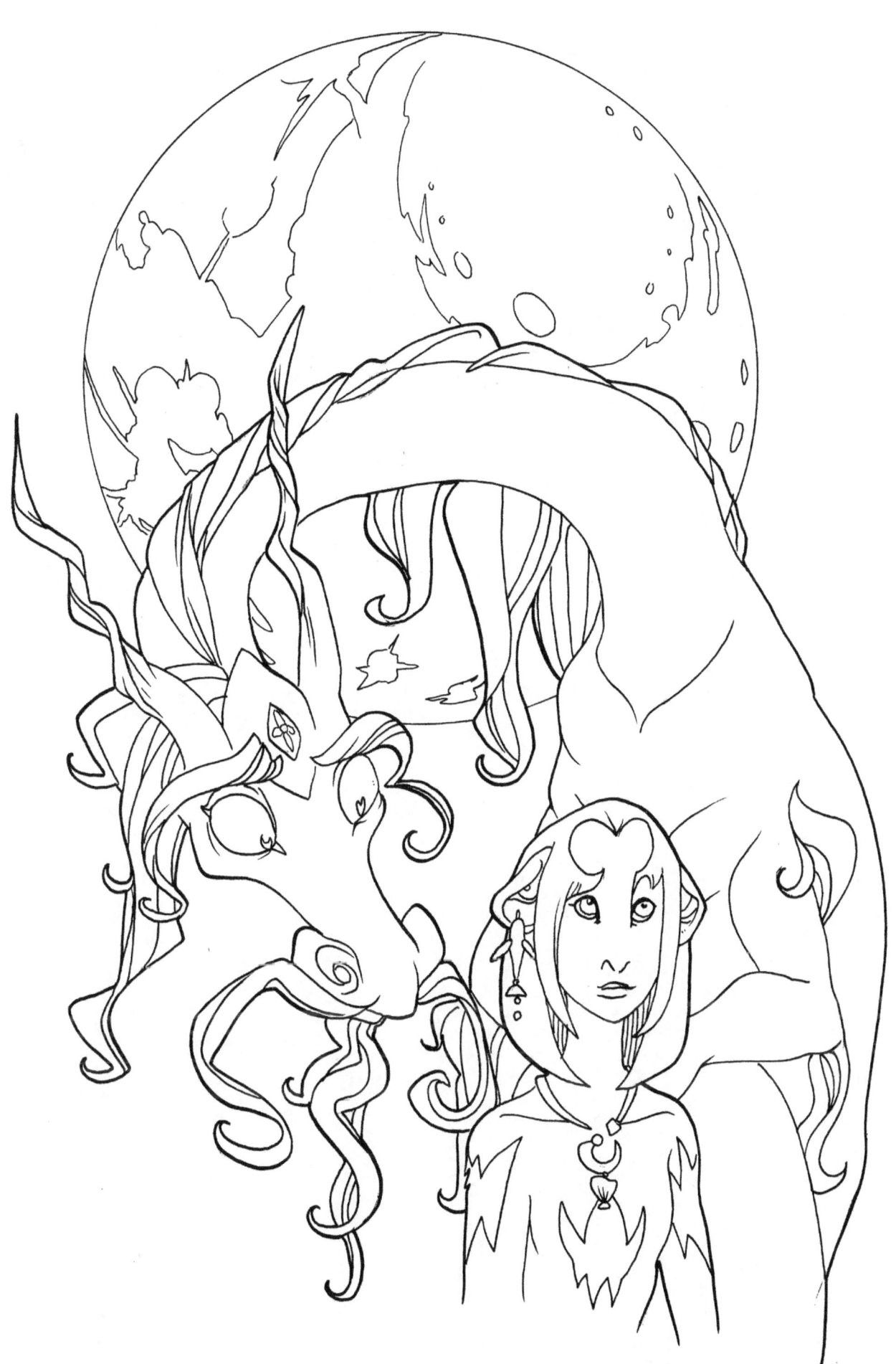

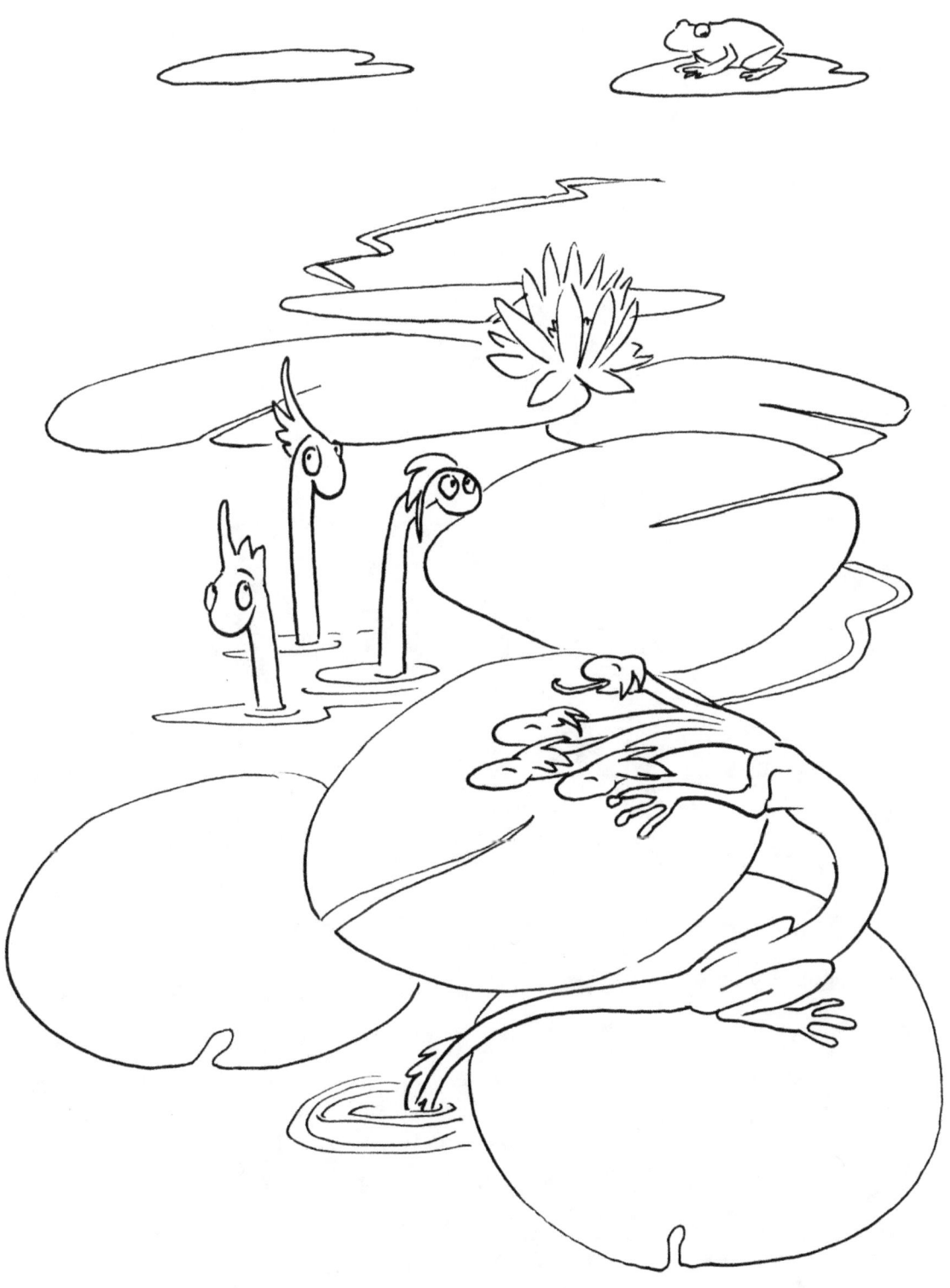

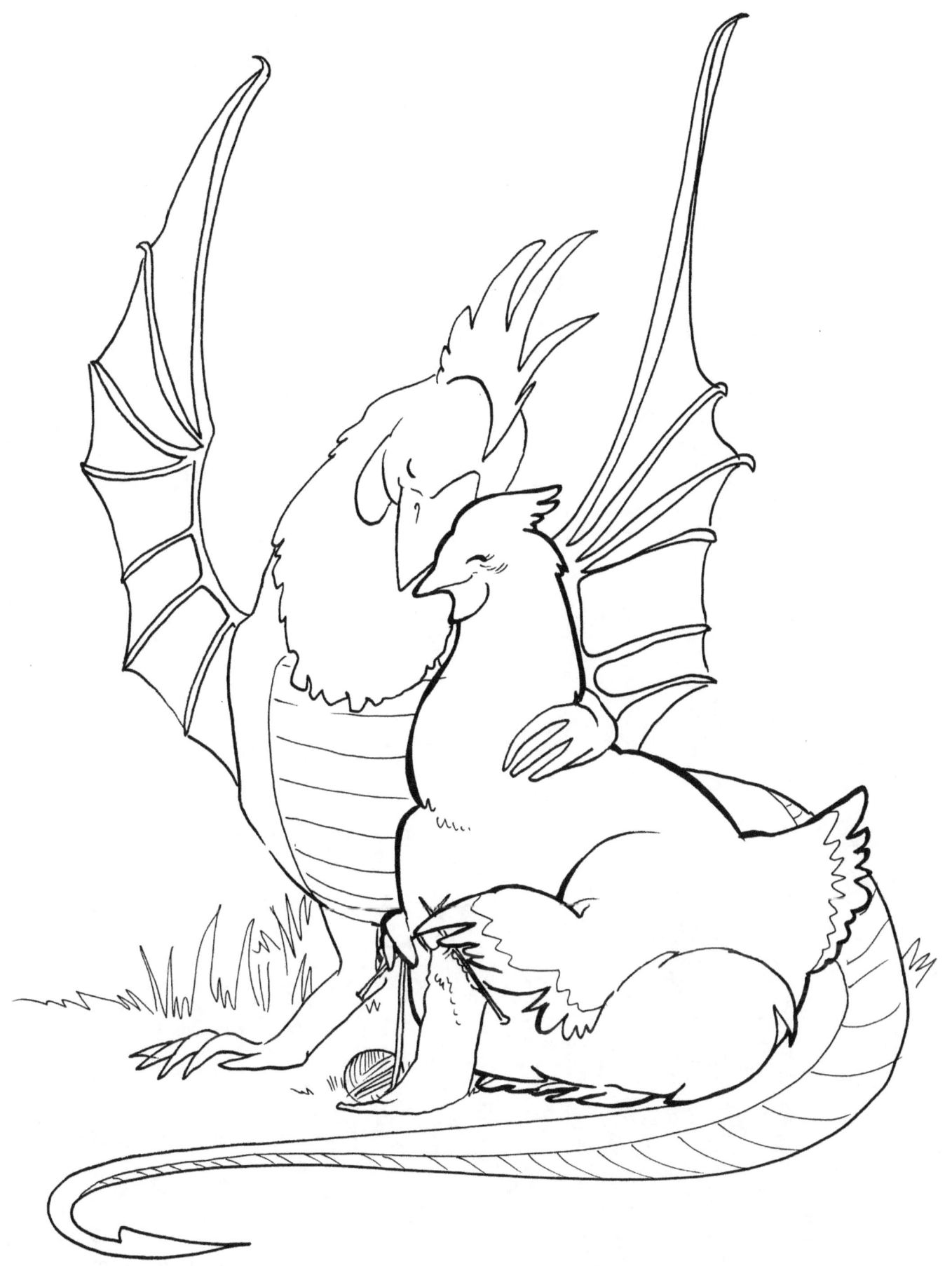

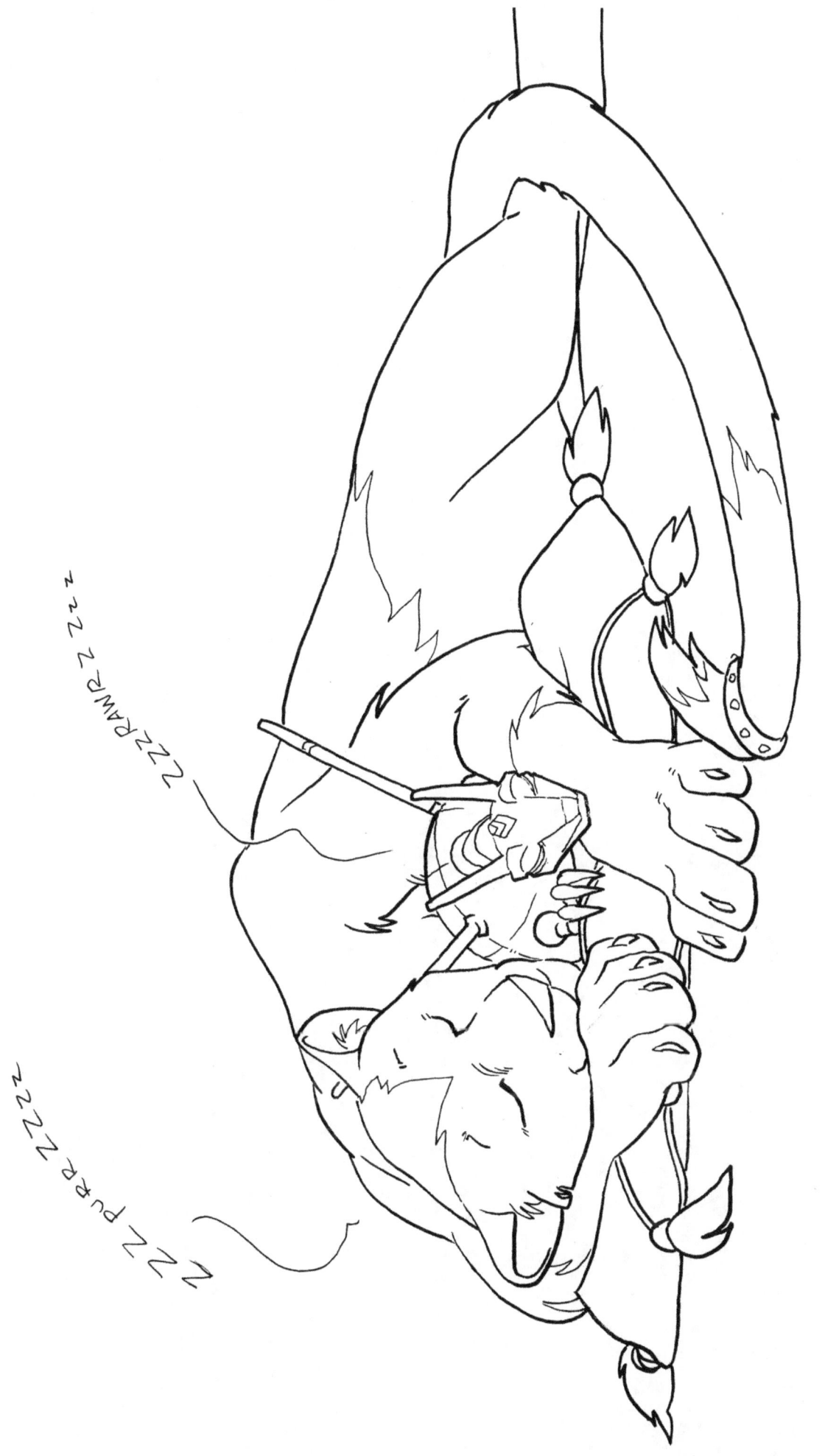

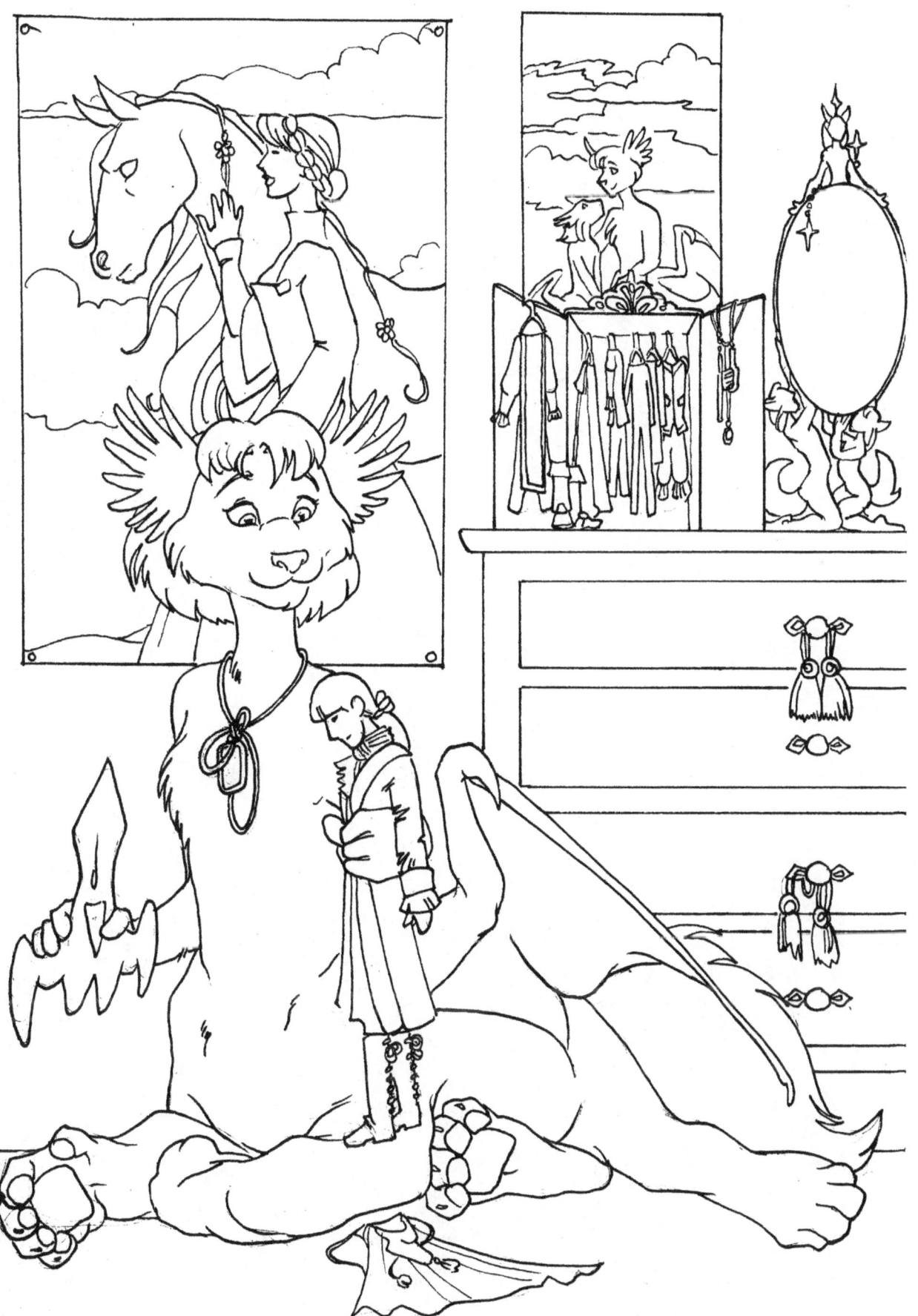

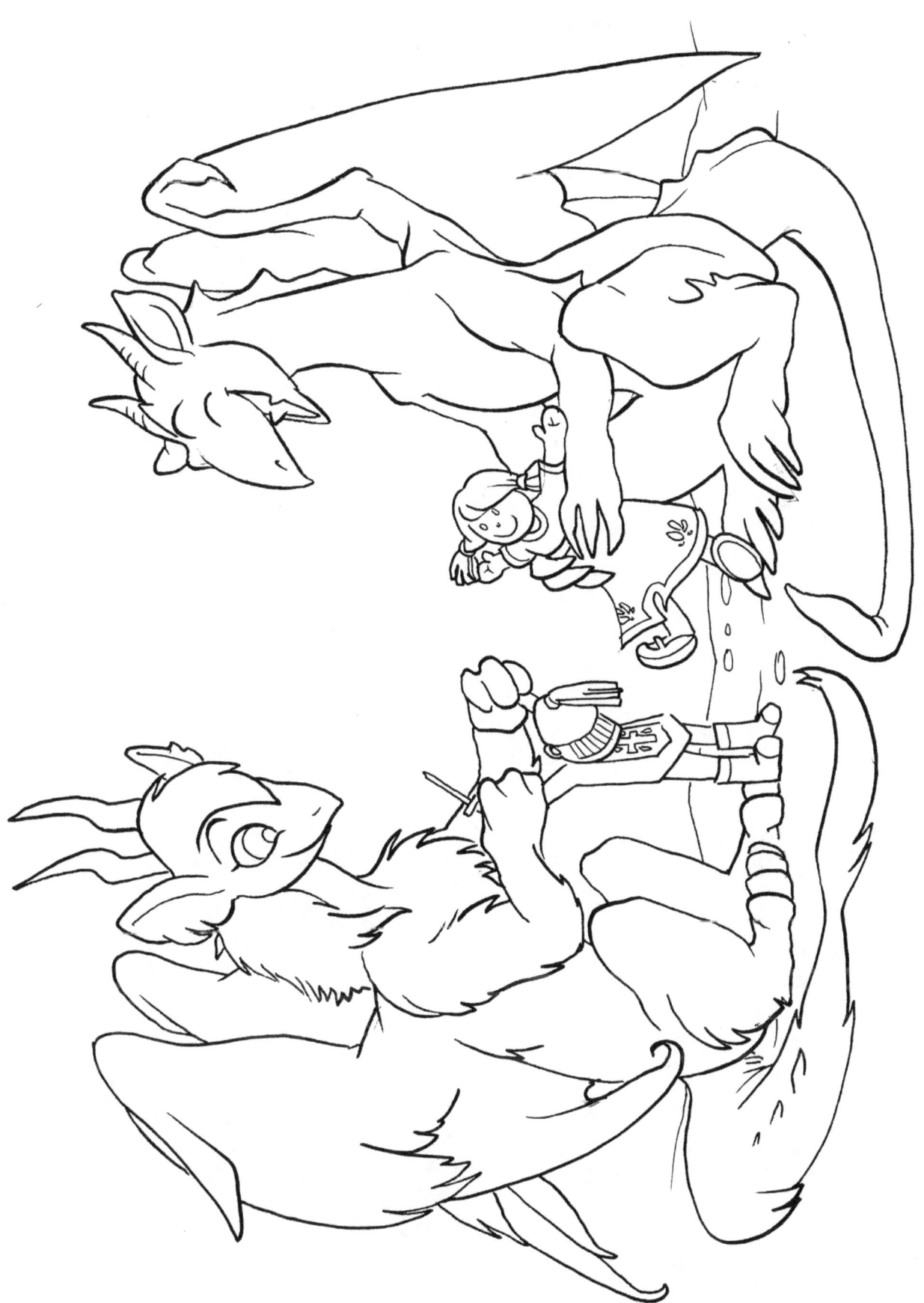

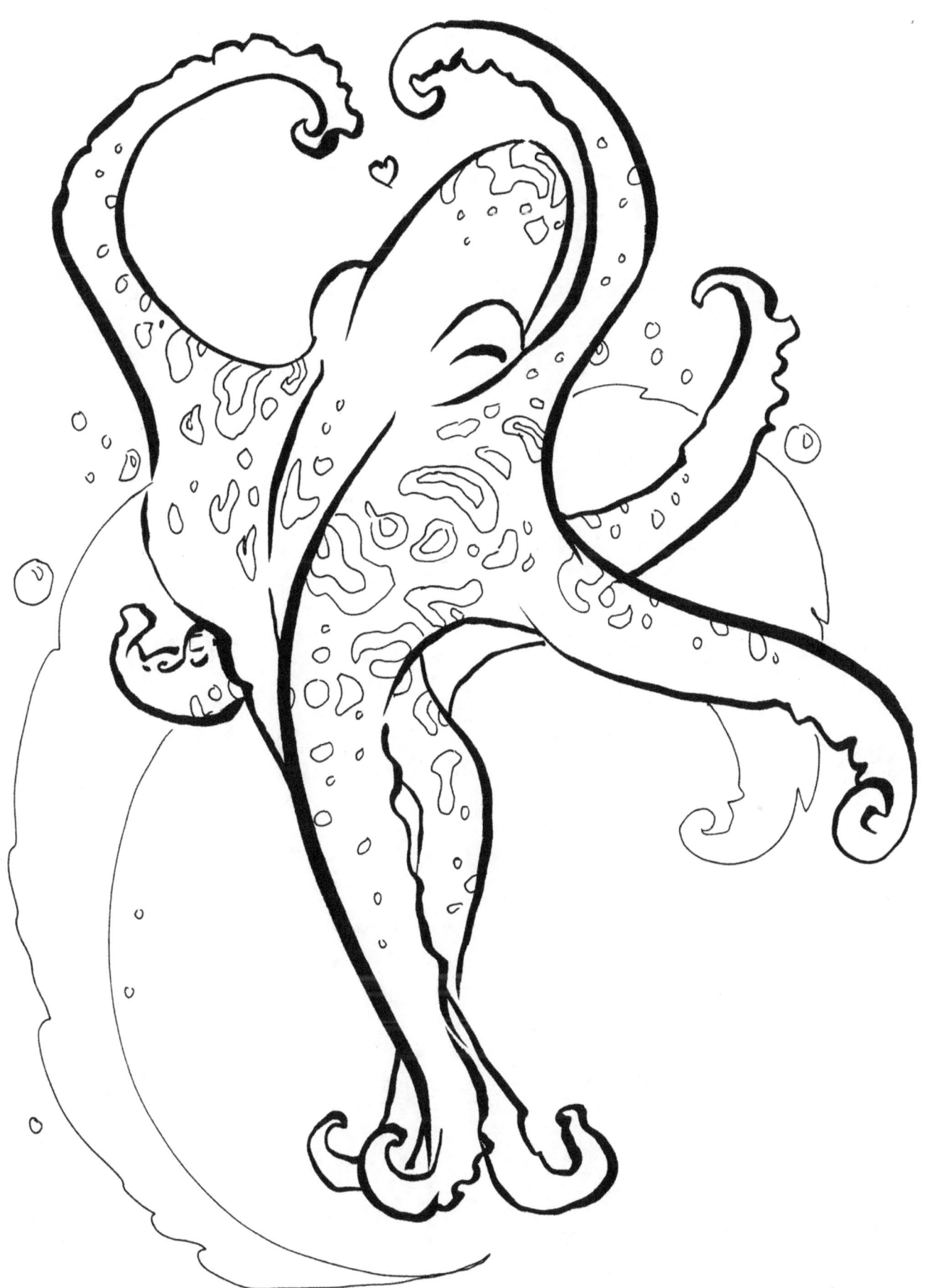

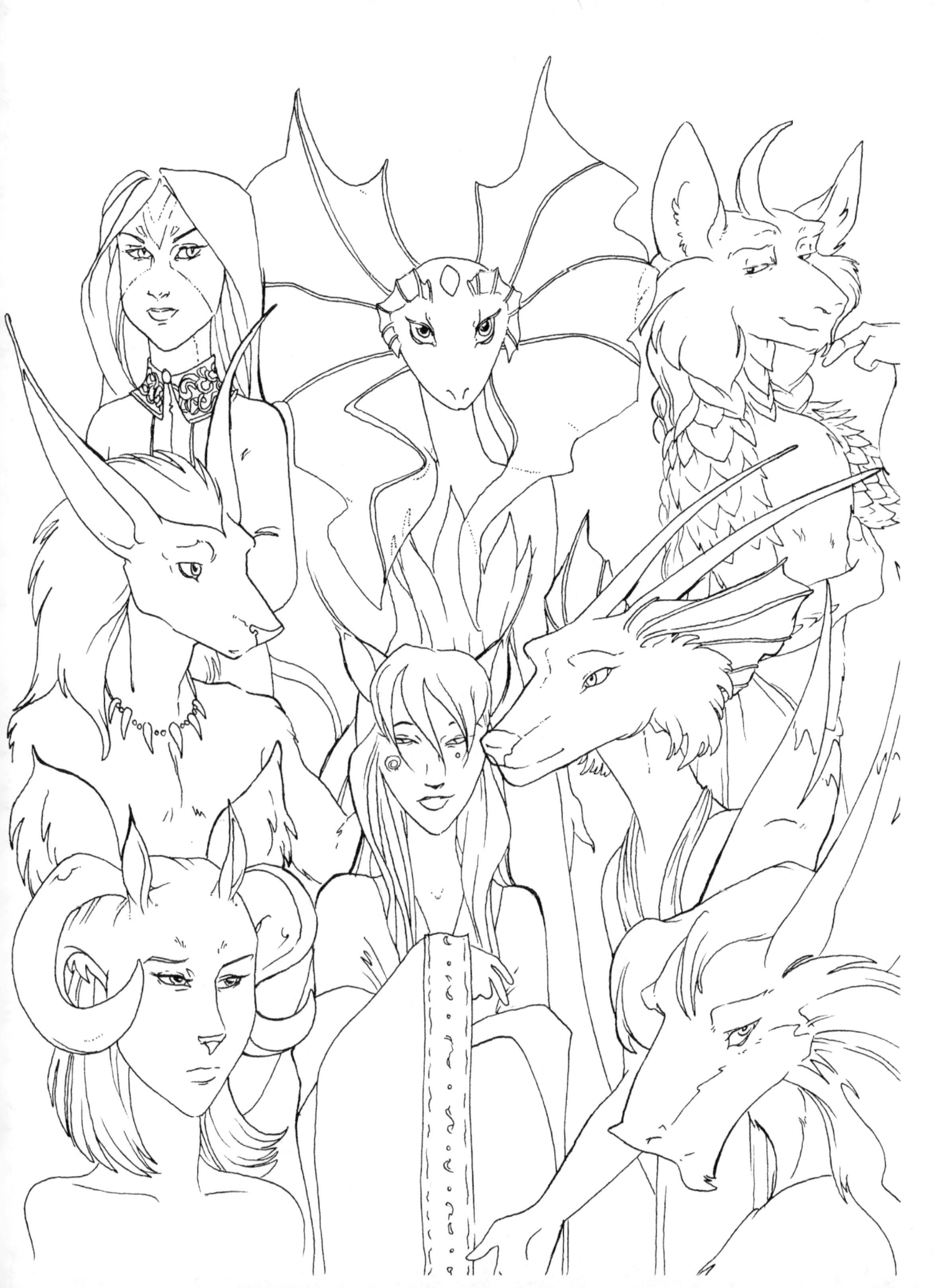

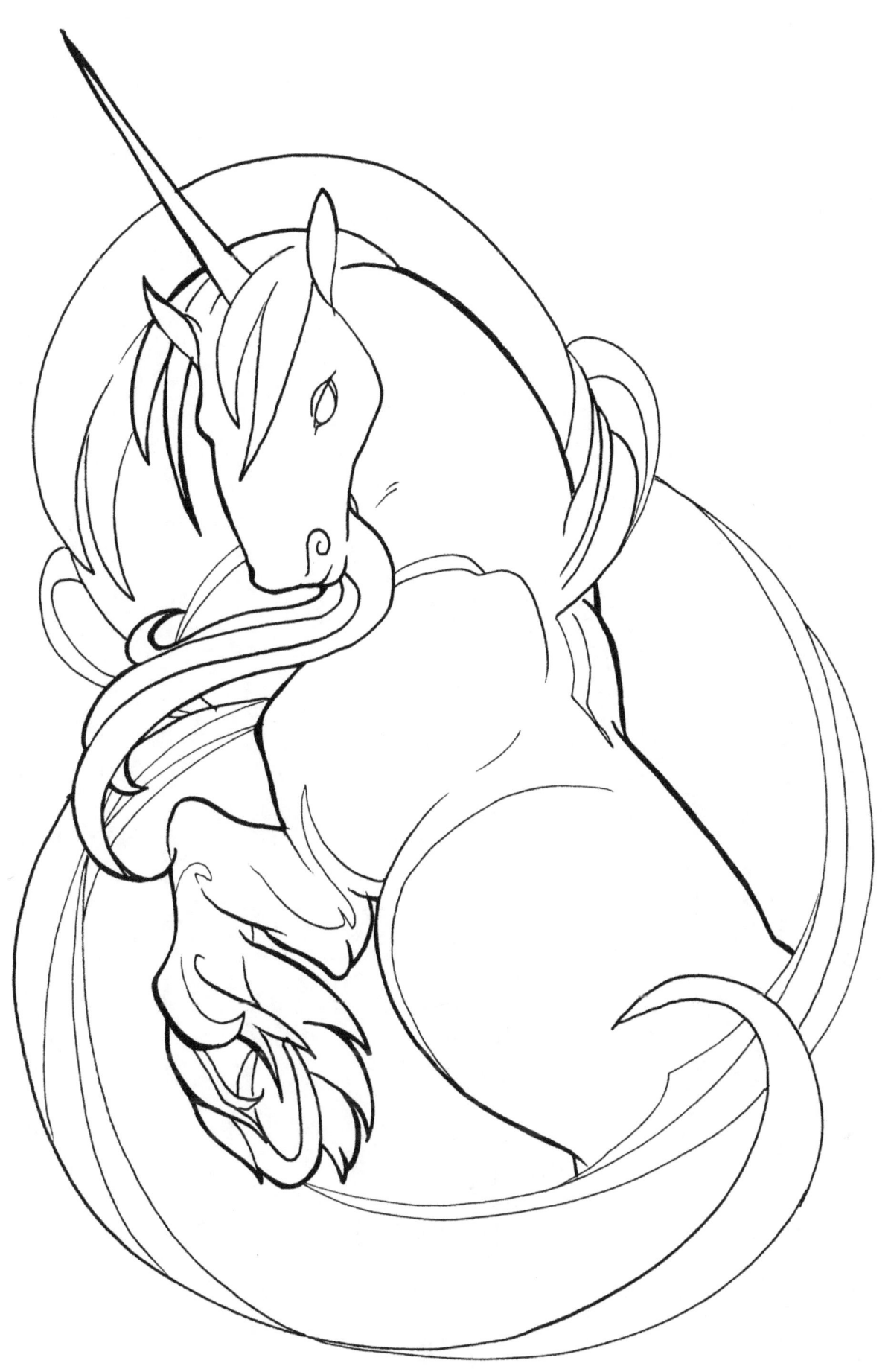

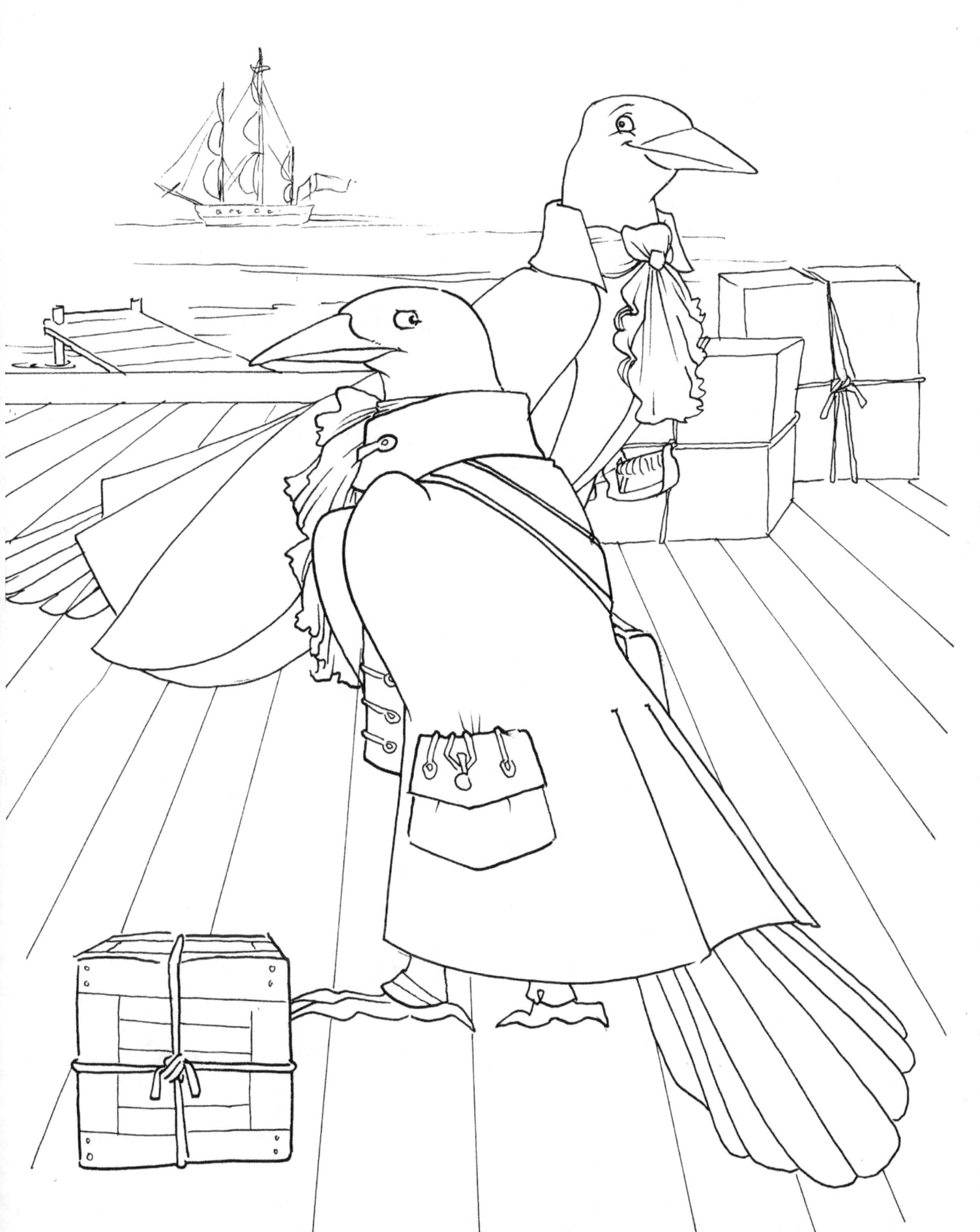

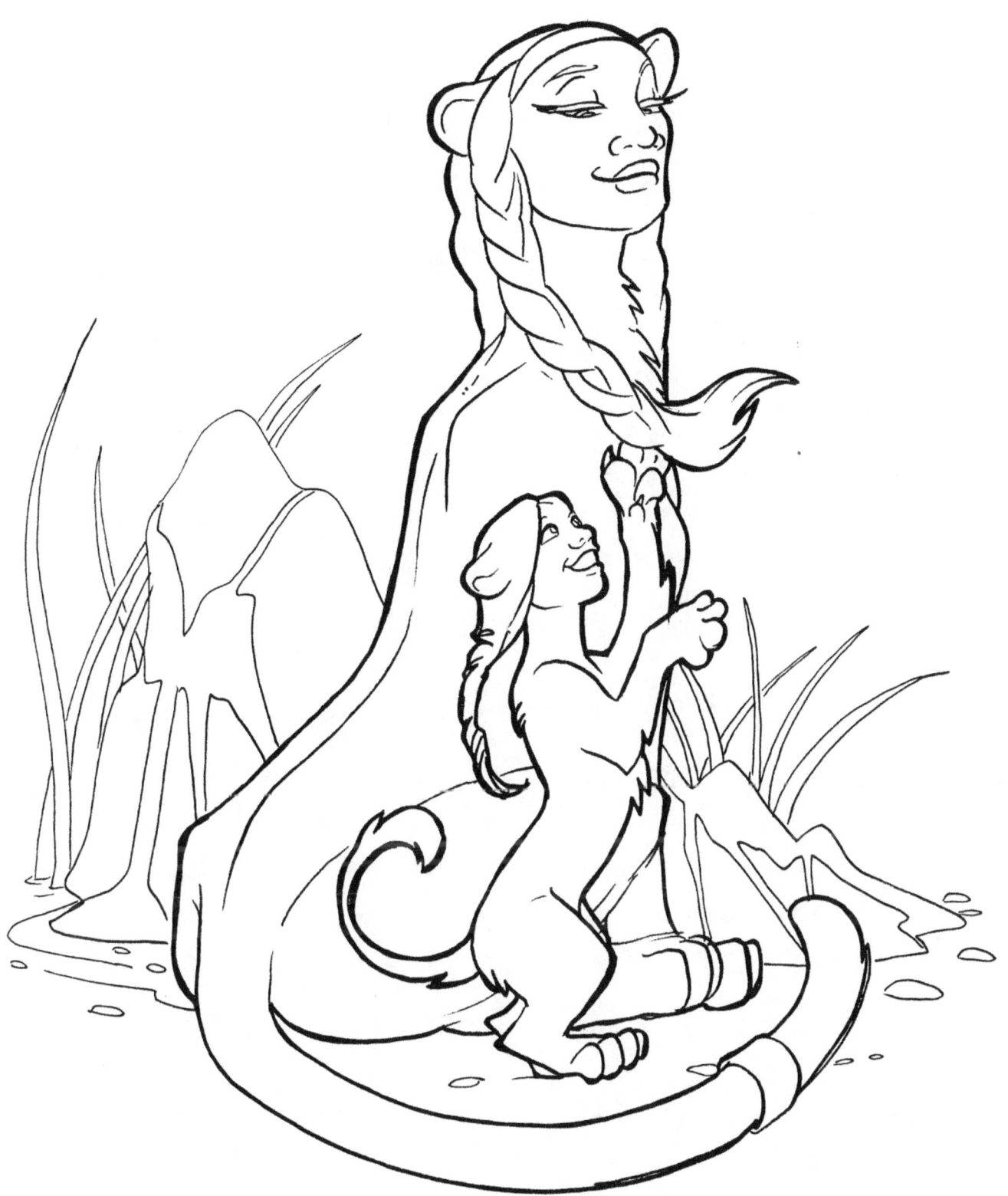

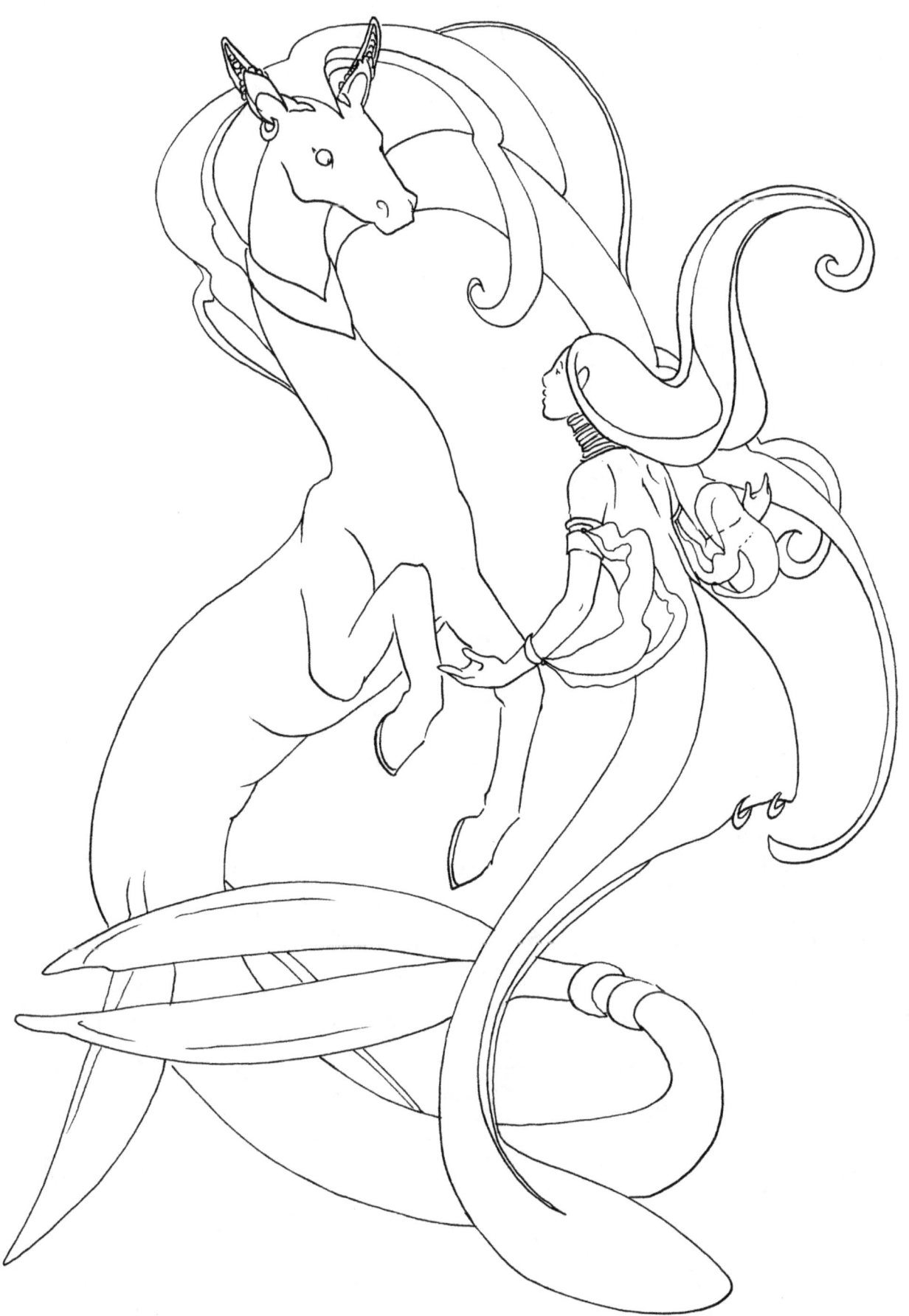

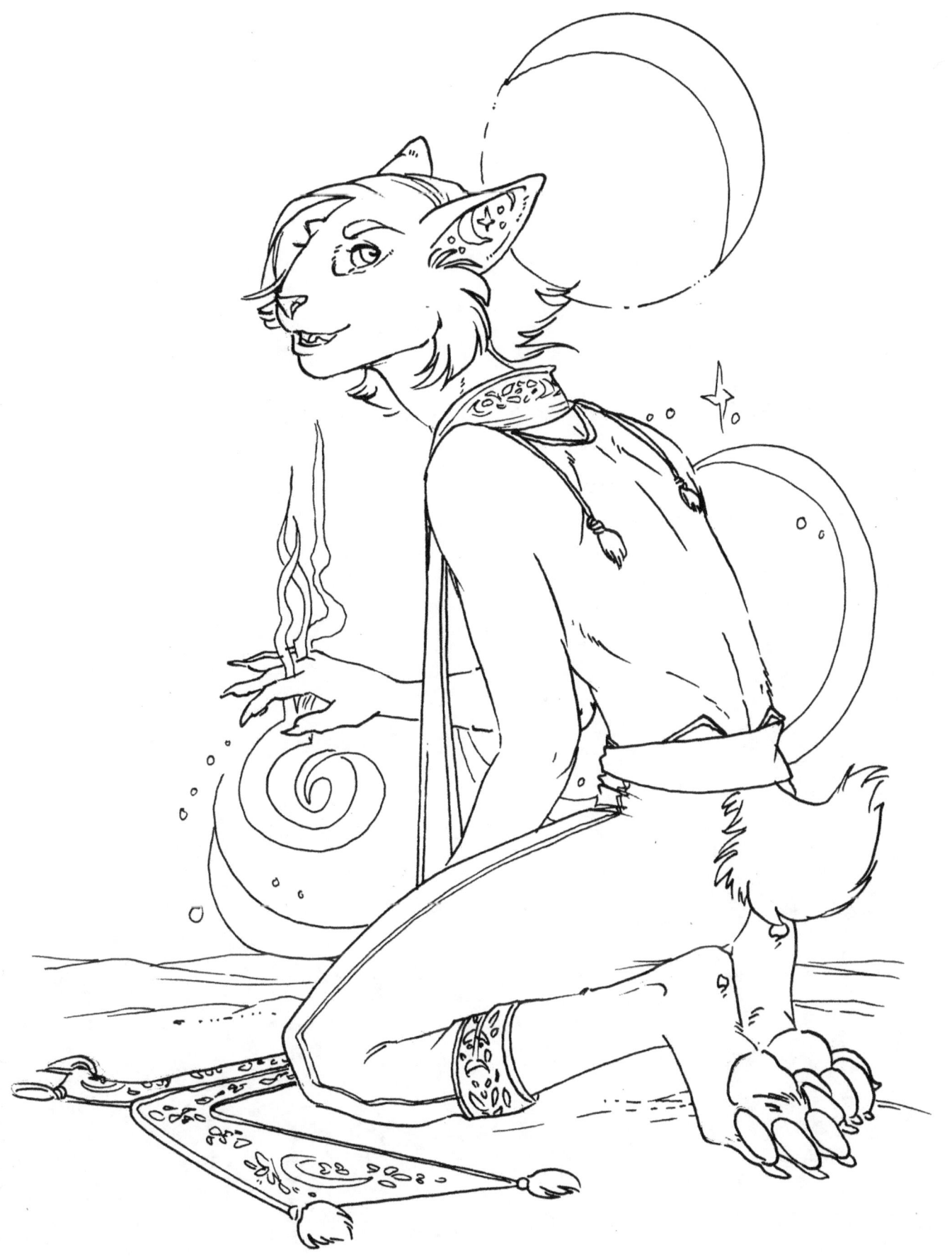

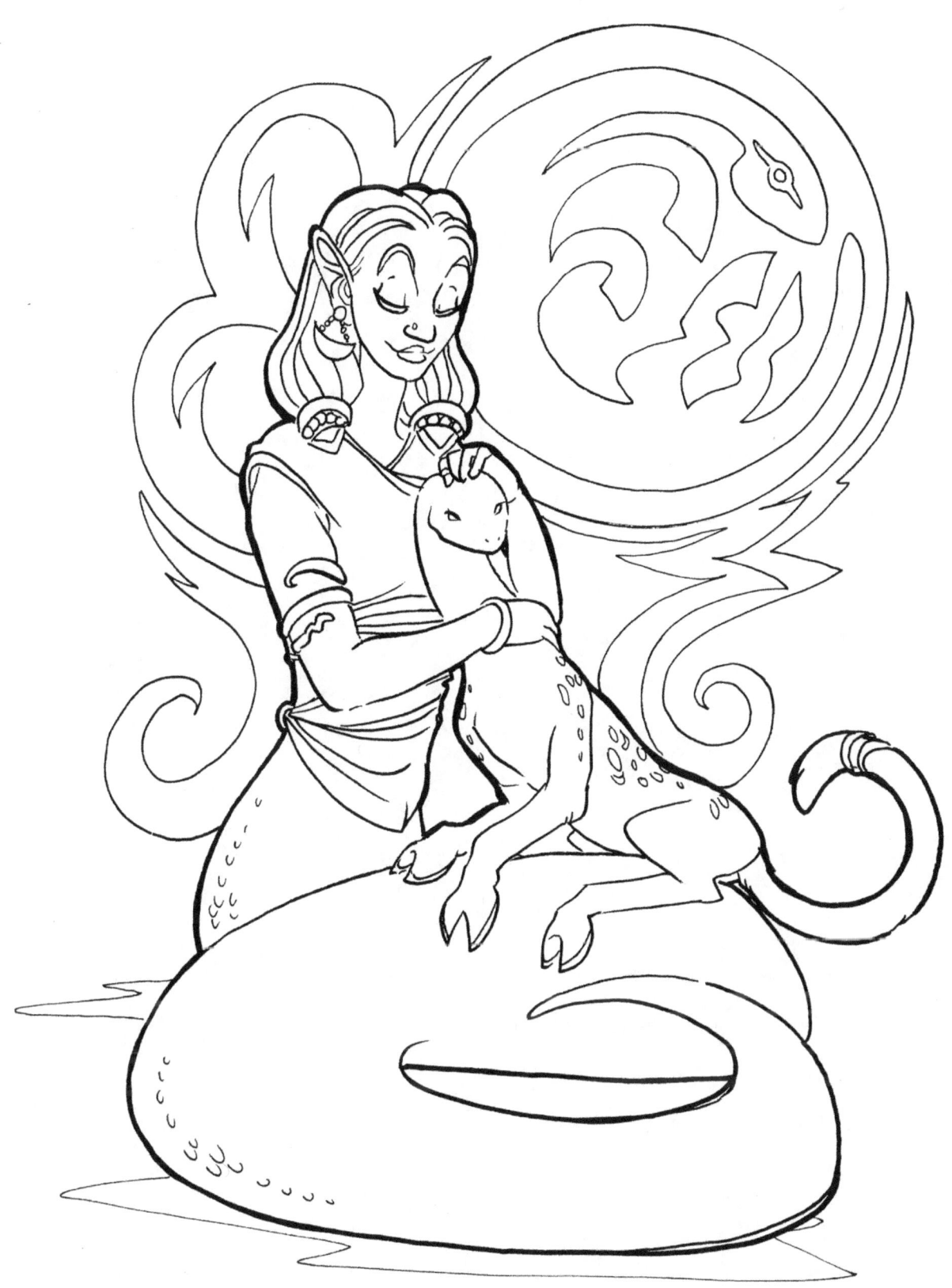

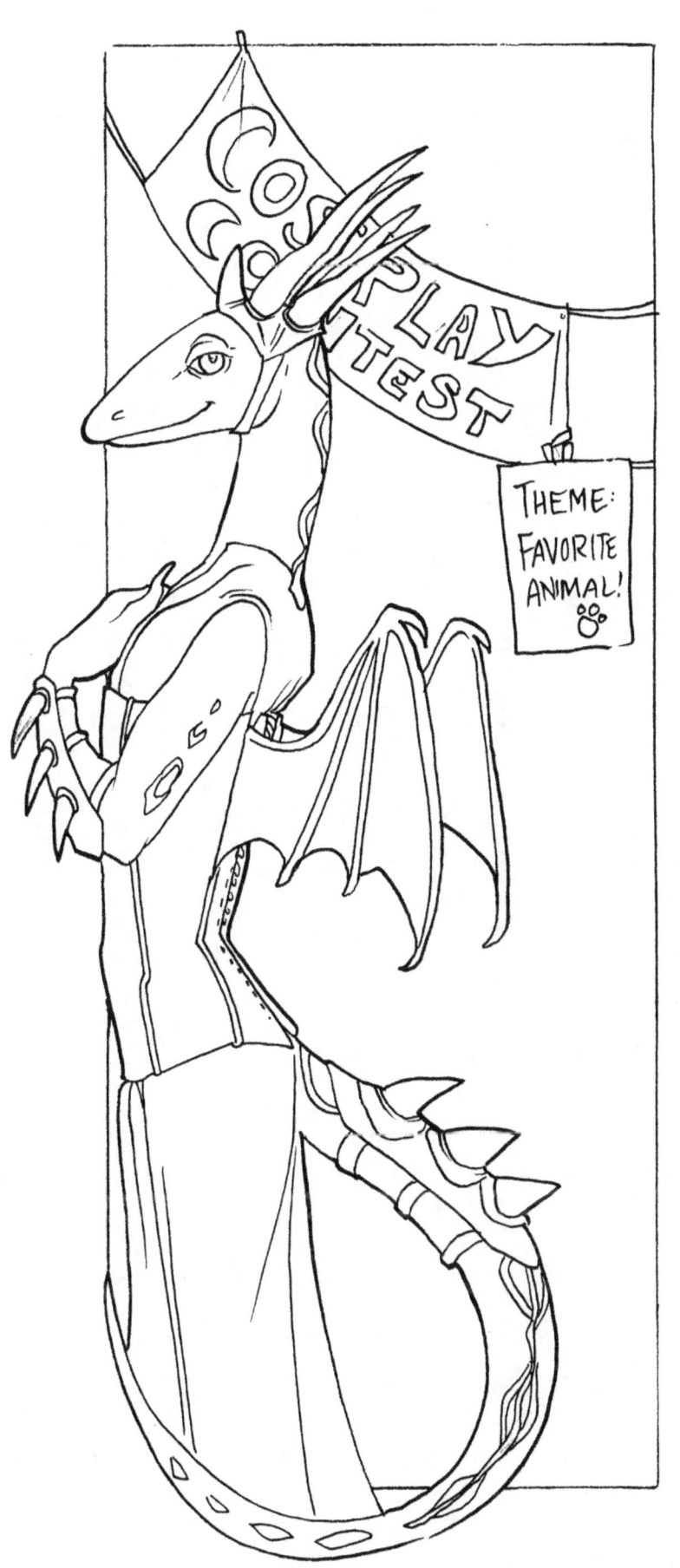

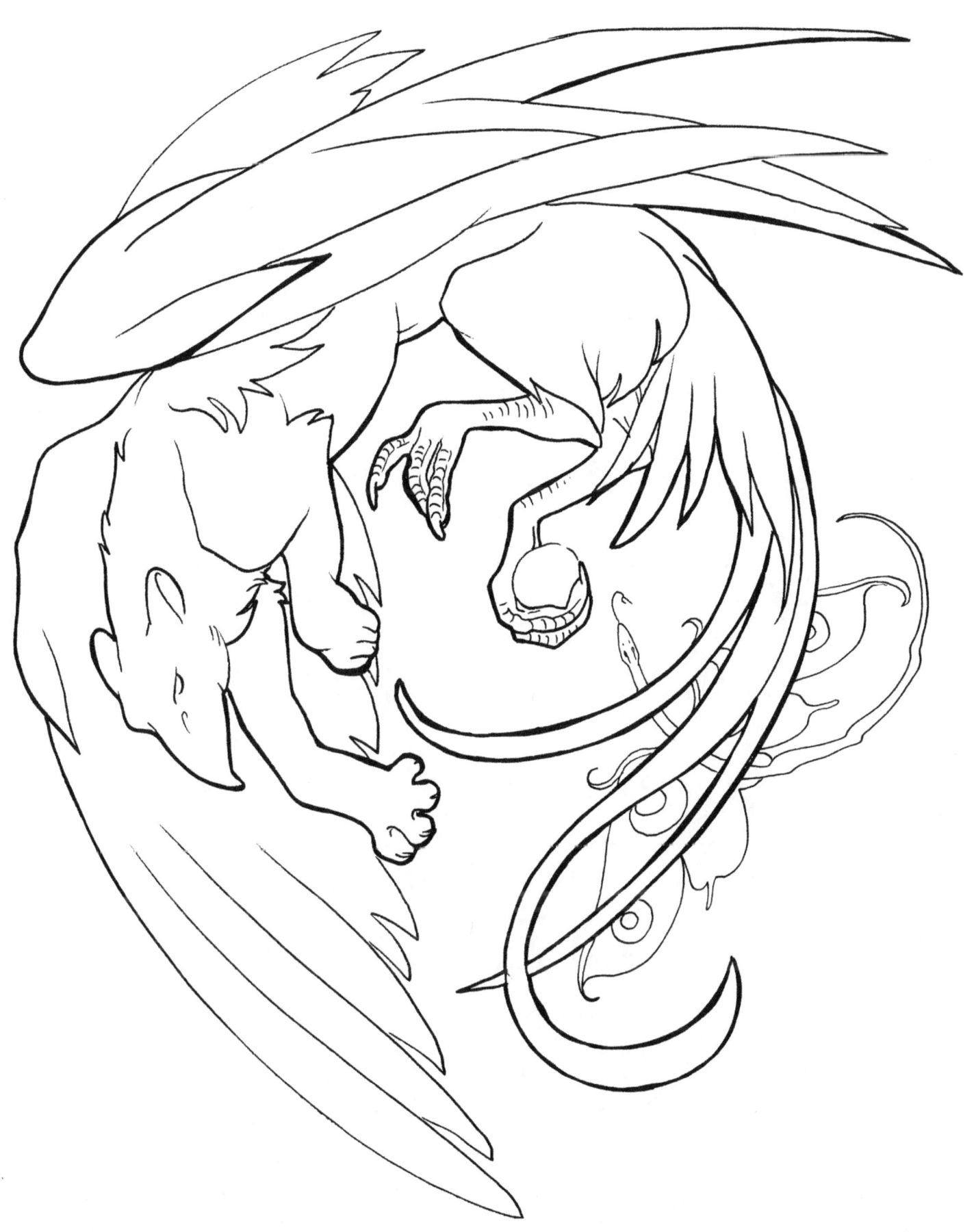

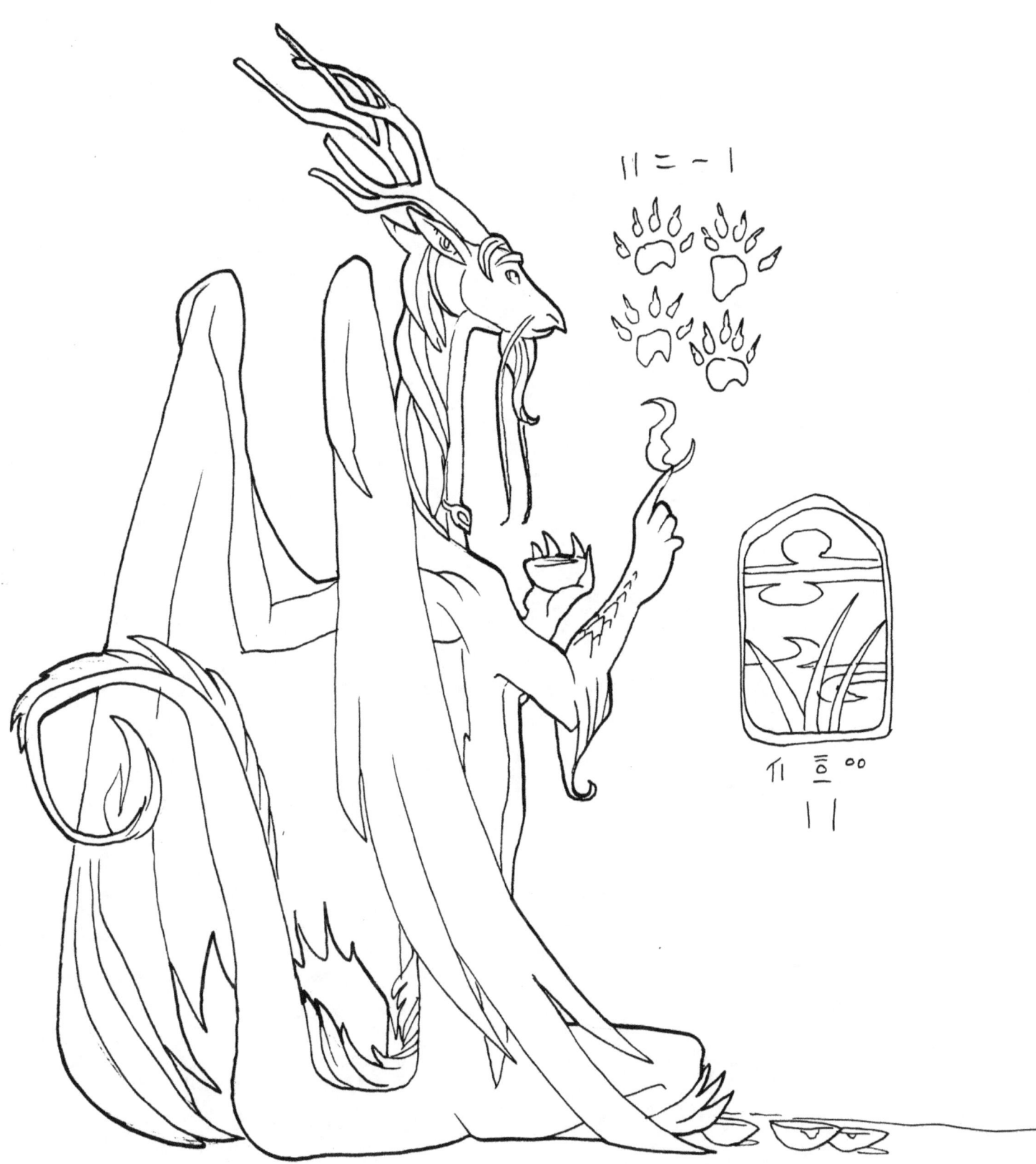

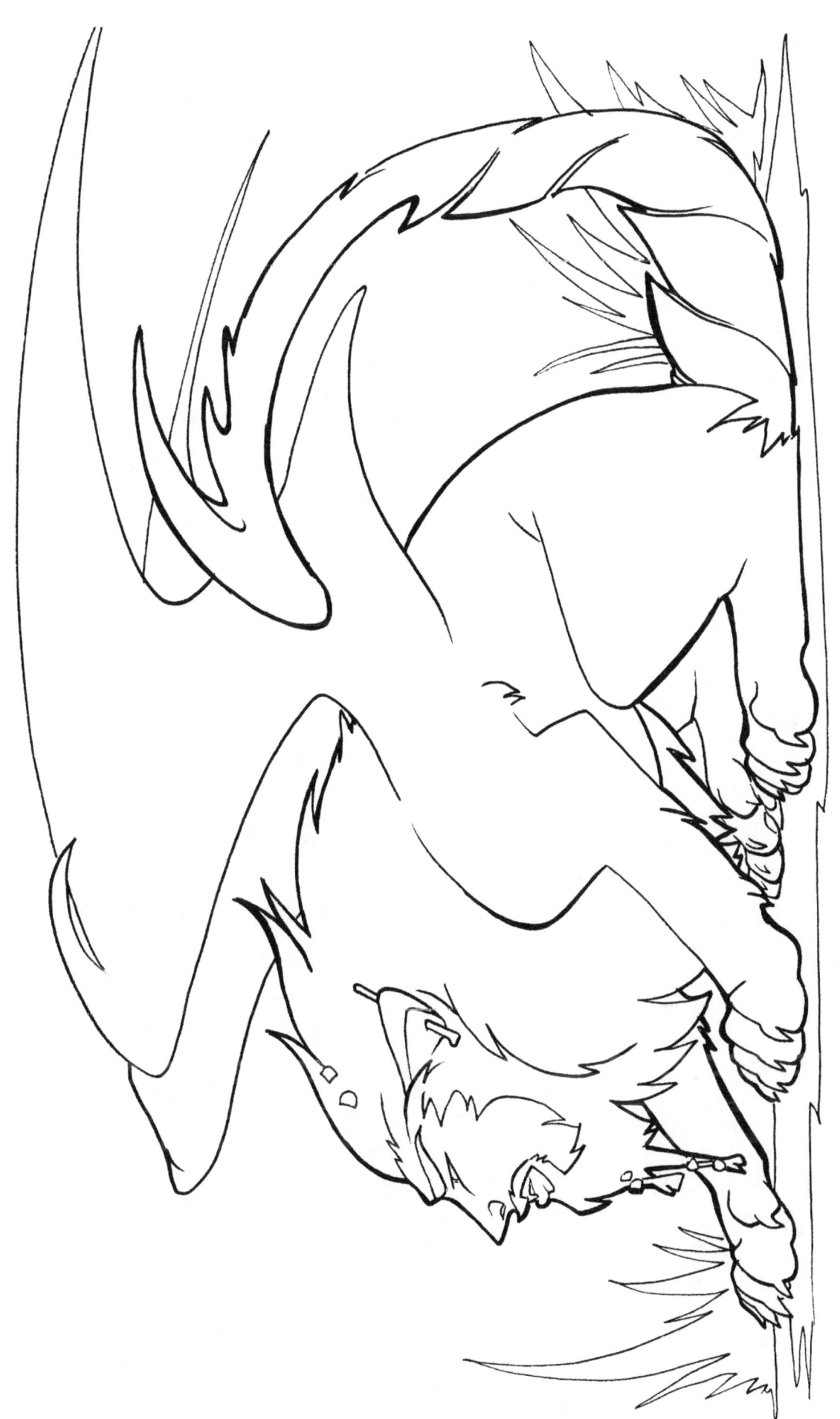

M.C.A. Hogarth is a storyteller who draws, and the author of over forty books of mostly fantasy, science fiction, and romance. Some of the creatures in this coloring book are from her various novels; if you'd like to try one, *Mindtouch* is her bestseller! She also writes children's books under the name Maggie Hogarth.

She makes coloring books to relax (and hopes you find them relaxing to use!); if you enjoyed this one, check out the others already available at online retailers:

Not in Need of Rescue: A Woman in Fantasy Coloring Book

Not in Need of Quests: A Men in Fantasy Coloring Book

The Jokka Coloring Book

The Laundry Dragons' Coloring Book Adventure!

And others forthcoming under the series name "Studio MCAH Coloring Books."

Thank you for buying! And enjoy!

mcahogarth.org
mcahogarth@twitter

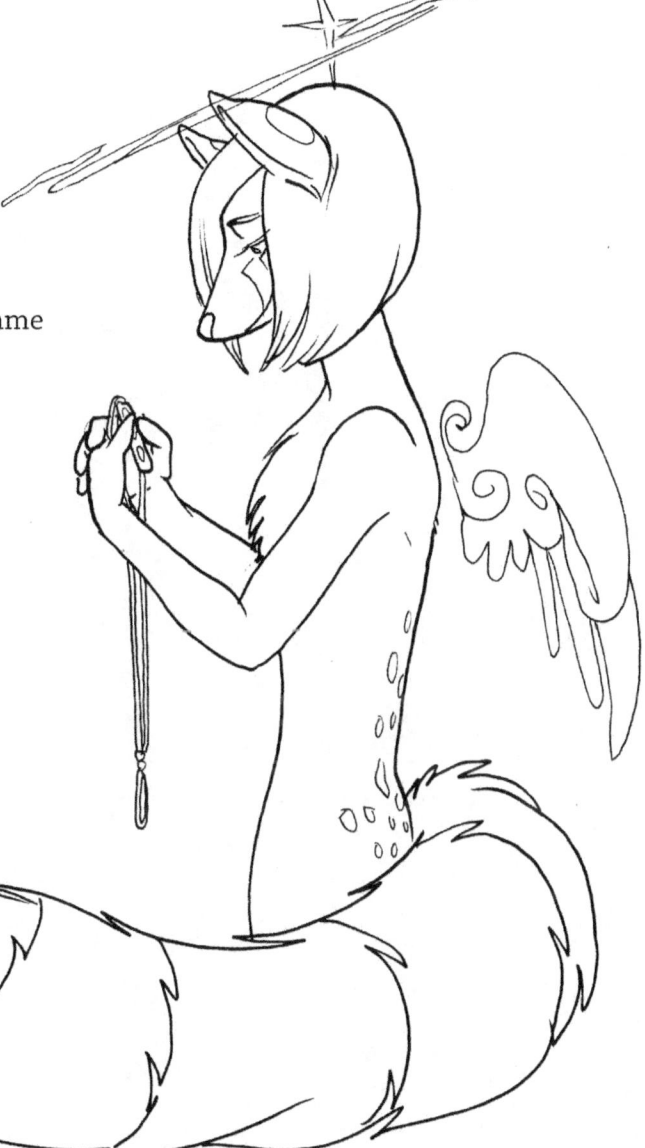

www.ingramcontent.com/pod-product-compliance
Lightning Source LLC
Chambersburg PA
CBHW080621180526
45168CB00007B/3005